META-BLACK: THEORY & PRACTICE

by
ROSIE LEE

Cover art: Rosie Lee, *Public School Complex*, 2018. © Rosie Lee.
Courtesy of the artist.

Brooks & Catlett Publishing

Library of Congress Cataloging-in-Publication Data

Lee, Rosie

Meta-Black : Theory & Practice / Rosie Lee.— 1st ed.

ISBN 978-1-7369350-1-9

Brooks & Catlett Publishing
Grand Rapids, MI 49505

Dedicated to my wife, son, and dreams.

Table of Contents

One

DRAW
FROM
INSPIRATION

Stuck

sitting in silence
boredom fills the air
curiosity laid to rest
a funeral procession occurs
in the corner

balled up ideas
roll pass discarded efforts
not wanting to be busy
but productive
a line is drawn
between wasting time and quitting

building upon doubt
blank stares and blank canvases
with money lower than feelings
feeding anxieties
swallowed whole
on an empty stomach

wallowing away at torn paper
led to believe
inspiration has forsaken me
affirmations transcribed
on napkins once used
to wipe away poems
written as scripture

Starting Place

poems written as scriptures
held together by pencil and paper
words stand by trial and error
here to bear witness
language is an infinite course
the finish line
exists as twists and turns
becoming figure eights

Manuscript

becoming figure eights
seeing life through symbol and form
wet my palette
color me love
paint my insides a retrospective
squeeze turpentine out of my skin
with brushstrokes of fire
burn my masterpieces
exhibit me
on graffiti walls
spill my heart onto life's canvas
sign my name in blood
instead, use number two pencils
to erase all traces of my existence
held sacred
by the sworn tongue
draw on the strength of the written

Write/Right

Draw on the strength of the written
ink spills
lines form letters
letters take up space
space spills into words
words yield compositions
left with unfilled desires
prepared, vulnerable and naked

Exhibition

prepared, vulnerable and naked
waited a year for this
to be put on display
critiqued and criticized
reviewed and curated
private tours guided by strange voices
telling all of my idiosyncrasies
no indiscretions, just statements
what I do and how I do it
and in the end
what do I get
another chance to be exposed
in there I have nothing to hide
shipped and packaged
waiting for my departure
left with no choice
returning to empty space
and blank walls
the only thing left of me

Monolithic

The only thing left of me
exists outside of difference
we are not the same
sameness isn't our color
shaded by boxes
we are gifts

we are not the same
sameness isn't our struggle
labels don't define us
we are art

we are not the same
sameness isn't our purpose
not institutionalized by your buildings
we are free

we are folk and fine
art made by outsiders, public and graffiti
we are all many things
but we are not the same

Graffiti Writers

But we are not the same
on canvas buildings
black and brown thespians

wrote love poems
with spray cans in hand

they started a revolution

Social Media

They started a revolution
digitized freedom by using bots and algorithms
then caused Bluetooths to grind to a halt
where chatter sounds the alarm

for the masses to run in a field of exclamation marks
a great expression of excitement and overly used quotes
why can't I share love until it is viral and breaks
the internet?

scroll through emojis until I reach a selfie of God
connect with friends in clouds
saving memories until I reach Heaven
no autocorrect, because mistakes don't allow me to pause and place
commas,

reflecting in four-inch screens are brail like dreams
browse around a globe as if the world is at my fingertips
megabyting cookies and snacking on computer chips
trolling Intel and swiping what is left of me
all of this to be liked

Paper

All of this to be liked
a place to gather thoughts
tell encrypted secrets
express the inner depths of self
express the imagination of God
grow history until it bends into time
control lines, forms, and shape the unknown

oh, the places found in thoughts
not uttered but whisked and pushed around
flowing throughout space
curious to see how you looked in abstraction
vulnerable as you pour out you
and sift through fears and insecurities

language is communicated in color
soon to be covered up with light
and the way shadows fall on the crease
folding away the seriousness found in play
it's the nuance and subtlety in the voice
so many others voice their opinions

they, too, see the potential in knowing
freedom to share truth
critique doubt and everything in between

the thrill is defining love

passion trails along
wanting to be acknowledged
and rightfully so
because of the passion of creating sound

words, the power to speak reality
no this is not a dream
not to be confused with fairy tales
narratives of things larger than life
then again, you are make believe
made to believe the lie and truth as one
selected for its texture and appeal to the eye

what lies beneath its surface?

it was created for you to draw on
paint a new day
send to the heavens as a plane
soak up tears
construct formulas
hold dear and seal with a kiss
claim it as your own
pass along as a note
whatever you decide to do
go beyond the margins

Lines

Go beyond the margins
from point A to B

and everywhere in between
light will exist

and everywhere in between
lines are drawn

where life meets death

Wash

Where life meets death
to be whitewashed away
dressing up flesh tones
applying whitening crème
as if Gesso could cover up black culture
stick to what comes natural
melanin drippin'
light from the sun
painted black, turning dark brown
ambers spark shades of sierra
sepia, copper like and ochre
until yellow medium hue, bone dry
sketching anatomy with charcoal
ready to catch fire
never watered down

Shade

Never watered down
unapologetically authentic
can't smear my black
in darkness you will appreciate my light
all that shineth in me
be mindful of where you stand

Pastel

Be mindful of where you stand
in fashion and on trend
the high value and low saturation blends
in circles and within circles

Be mindful of who you are
in fashion and on trend
not here to serve or entertain
in color and about our color

Be mindful of your light
in fashion and on trend
while *en vogue* or when your color fades
in house and color fields
be free

Mixed Media

Be free
the heart is a gathering place
where love
boils over into gumbo
soaked up
by an exodus of dreams
leaving behind
memories as artifacts
all to show
the medium is the message

Pencil Me In

The medium is the message
not one for words
when we met
I put all my imperfections on the table
instead of drawing conclusions

your remarks tattooed my ego
in between the lines, we were unparalleled

stories abound with each curve
tracing what makes us human
so far, with number two pencils
lead on a journey
can't erase our history

Sketch

Can't erase our history
go figure, drawing your anatomy
the naked eye and the bare naked truth
some copy while others trace along

Charcoal

Some copy while others trace along
char burn on pencils
hot stains on constitutions
black ash resurrected
draw upon the fingerprints of slaves
sketching freedom
for generations

the struggle is (con)temporary
can't match our will
ready to light a fire in ebony hearts
then, set everything ablaze
America will soon learn we *coal* as fuck

Smear

America will soon learn we coal as fuck
until our eyes shine diamonds
limestone sculptures
will never eclipse pyramids
in a campaign of lies
all colors mix into humanity

race is just that
a race
color is just that
pigment
a construct built for privilege

throw European dirt on our Asiatic names
they dug up Lucy
and covered up the truth
to be whitewashed away
our pharaohs and gods
replaced by Greek mythology
while museums display
the art of thieves
knowing there is Moor to see
a history of erasure

Trace

A history of erasure
doesn't transfer power
only transitions the inevitable

Gravity pulls the body into Earth
worms eat our remains
early birds rise with the sun
fly away with those ascending to Heaven

It is deeper than blood
and spreads faster than lies
finding legacy in those who came before

The mark making of the enslaved
etched in everything I write
draw upon their strength
for good measure
revolution will be our legacy.

Two

PAINT
WITH
PURPOSE

Neutral

black nights
white days
grey skies

black skin
white flesh
grey matter

black paint
white canvas
grey space

seen through
brown eyes

Frame of Mind

Seen through brown eyes
there is a reason to protest
riot and smash windows

for they have looted
tombs for our bodies
and our bodies of work
missing from walls
stolen and put on display
a collection of cultures
not your own

barbaric tactics
built their institutions
and they call themselves civilized
elitist and contentious
critique the poor and wretched

blessed are the framers
because we intend to burn this place down
maybe then you will have a new frame of mind
something to constitute other than me
hired only to protect your property
there is a difference between ruin and rebellion
we choose the latter

Modern Masters

We choose the latter
for being poor costs
unlike bottled up culture
sold at convenience stores
so naïve to think we'd fizzle out

now, everyone wants to buy black
instead of fool's gold
keep your pawnshops
and check cashing place
either you are the assailant or victim
you can't be both

they call on tradition
while we call for new standards
seated at the table
with an appetite for truth
we pull up a chair and square off
eating hand over fist
serving justice on good china
we laid down our hair
but not our guns

we're our best
when expressed in abstraction
space and form
in figure

with mask and quilts
(Gee's Bend)ing your ear
face the mirror
and all that you hate

time for the world to see
outside itself
oh, the things we buy into
on loan to the public
a collection of people, built on freedom
existing as the cornerstone
refusing to build
what you already ruined
if I am to recognize you as master
you must first see me as God

Sublime

You must first see me as God
converting to higher values of self
confused on whether to chase dreams
or simply be still
a greatness explored in the beyond
beyond measure and calculation
it is my nature to be creative
a birth right
because I am made up
both beautiful and ugly
made out of love
thought of as a notion
an expression
greater than plus signs
a savant and high priest
placing critique on divine things
escaping space
to be spiritual
going against physics
to exist as ALL
an aesthetic
where I'm in awe of me

I told the angels don't worry
I will toot my own horn
dance in the breeze
and with one fell swoop

blow down romantic visions of beauty
for we shall appear meta-black

Form and Figure

For we shall appear meta-black, in theory and practice
made in abstraction, her form and his presence
the essence of us
shall remain undefined

Watercolor

The essence of us shall remain undefined. Organic in shape, fluid in form. With brush in hand, give chase. As inequities soak into paper. Drink from the pool of inspiration. Pour out my soul on canvas. For creativity shall thirst no more.

Open Call for Women

For creativity shall thirst no more
she exists here
between revolving doors and glass ceilings
although bound to her gender
her art pushes boundaries
no welcome mat
before she enters
they called and she answered
unfortunately, not wanted and undervalued
she was shooed away
asked, only to be seen not heard
only seen not displayed
only seen not collected
only seen not known
for being more than a woman

Let the Paint Dry

For being more than a woman
time waits for no man
therefore, be virtuous
when the dust settles
endure adages about hard lessons
trust discernment
become sold on the idea of unfinished business
emptied out on the journey
fulfilled by the dues you paid
owe no one an explanation
when it's all said and done
there comes a time
you must walk away
let the paint dry

Flesh Tones

Let the paint dry
eyes closed
color blind by the process
smear on black
from the abyss
a dab more yellow than tooth decay
built up on gritty teeth
a pinch of rich purple
similar to dark lips
that inhale and exhale Newport cigarettes
paint on blues
with Mississippi mud
red like numbers
in poor people's bank accounts
can't forget about the pink
juicier than a peach
squeezed between hot cocoa thighs
apply milky white and brown from tits
breast used to nurse a nation
hues used to build "they" shit
a pure grey
sewn together with ol' folk hair
you know
salt and pepper
and the collard greens be deeper than taste buds
planted in my roots....shoot
let light fade away, a self-portrait

set in the sun
a paint chip off the old block
crinkled and weathered
I am more than pigment

Print

I am more than pigment
even my dreams need room to breathe
give me some space
as I calculate my value
come appraise your worth
with politics and commissions
heal your ego
with public scars
as you take your cut
money affects the bottom line
here is where you sign
your name

everything has become overly processed
never compromise your dignity
such a huge price to pay
repeat to find a cheaper form of me
myself, I'm a one of one
labeled original

Color Theory

Labeled original
white is right
black don't crack
yellow good for math
red always comes in last
brown cuts green
unless it's too clean
green backs are the American Dream
blue supposed to protect and save
purple hearts for the brave
all colors of the rainbow means gay

Color Wheel

All colors of the rainbow means gay
except blacks and whites don't mix
is the race fixed
proliferated thoughts
connecting dots
waiting for someone to draw the line
about fact, fiction, and truths
the theory of color

Abstraction

The theory of color
a circle of life squared away in riddles
I used to theorize truths as myths
outside the lines, I draw attention to the rules
then make a B-line
until it is no longer a figure
all to make a point
there is no such thing as definitive

maybe, the light in color is perfect
then again, after I Gesso paint
and tape irregular sides
the idea of it
will look familiar
not of this world
possibly something imagined

and they say there is nothing new under the sun

the magic of it
can reach the end of why
it never ends
still, we keep coming up with
the science of it
not the mathematics in it
basking in its glory
its wonder

its depth
I push beyond its boundaries
of passion and love
this is where I begin to form art

Composition

This is where I begin to form art
performing as ring master
filled with an audience
of critics and wild animals
eaten by the lionhearted
trampled by the elephant in the room
their curiosity typically gets the best of them
no need to play it safe
paint the very thing they want to see
but deny

Foreground

Paint the very thing they want to see
but deny
up close and personal
their black skin brought onlookers
so, they were told
proceed to the *blackground*
told they didn't belong, except in negative space
told, in the background
they would find their place
a section
colored strictly for them

Oil

A section
colored strictly for them
void of water and fire
in order for linseeds to grow
I bury my bones
and empty everything out in the soil
where images begin to arise
out of black fields

Landscape

Out of black fields
in between black rage and black joy
and the wonder found
in black girl magic
a welcoming space created for freedom
there is no need to apologize for being black
because you exist
for no other reason than to be
what you want
what is needed
without explanation
where was I?

Minimalism

Where was I
less is enough
using words sparingly
not a lot to say
at a loss for words
not quite finished
mind blank

Monochromatic

Mind blank
in the presence of white noise
black sounds vibrate
depth and range
vocals color harmony
a collective consciousness
march in sync to protest
that which has been whitewashed
Greek statues and the likes
an erasure of color
applying Gesso to so-called mistakes
when white is the standard
everything tastes bland

Still Life (Strange Fruit)

Everything tastes bland
fruits and vegetables
harvesting soup for the soul
stomach grown full of promise
in this art world
fed their crumbs
some of us want a seat
decolonize your tableau and museums
classic hegemony

historic and systemic
we are not timid
moved to paint death
there should be no peace
for your walls
can't keep us out
demanding entrance
into your establishment
for I am
a living work of art

Portraits

A living work of art
a muse
amused by the concept
thoughts bleed on paper
as we free ourselves from ourselves
thoughts escape the mind into mere expression
see inside the soul
where remnants of clairvoyance
mask the poet's face
up in smoke
our youth disappears
left with memories
of regret and toil

I didn't choose to be here, I was chosen
in between joy and pain
is a place I call home
nothing lasts forever, not even time
experience is temporary, in space
so, fuck everything that was and couldn't be
couldn't be
because
I was not chosen to be
more than my potential

am I the mad man you see
or just plain mad

my curiosity has gone mad
for I seem to find questions
not answers
a revolt
you ask me not to speak of
a revolution
you don't want to hear from
this is what happens
when questions begin to form
an existence all their own
no path arrives at the right answer
just an alternative
of what exists for many
back to freedom and forward thinking
they call it progression

but it is difficult to trust what they say
don't sleep
for we
the new generation of free thinkers
are conscious
we just have our eyes closed
for we
can't forget to daydream
when old souls in young bodies
meet wise minds and childish grins
hand-outs and hands up
the voice of the people
has grown silent
what do you predict in the future

happy meals and toy grenades
feelings ain't nothing to play with
bite the hand that feeds you
and the ear you hear with
listen to the vibrations, *be steel*
try not to bend
reverberating sound
from knuckles on tables
a drum call to the sonic youth
and middle aged freaks
growing into cynical farts
waiting for our shit to drop
we are bringing the funk back baby
we're having church in theater boxes
where artists pop out like clowns in cars
I'm charged and in shock
from our global sound
screaming at the canvas
making a mockery of our expressions
a mirror
reflecting the critiques
of a pretentious world
look, there goes our culture
in hash tags and trends
uploaded to a cloud

let's hug it out
with the three headed monster
me, myself and I
no fairytales and no lullabies

just the hard truth
the only obstacle worth climbing
plus, the cliff hangers add drama
to the book of has beens and have nots
making connections to the dots

I tie knots
in the laces of those
taking the road less traveled
the wool used to cover my eyes
I used to knit street art
on corners
to warm the homeless
a way to give back
blanket statements
and stick figure it to the man

starving for attention
food for thought is being valued
duck and cover, a strange twist to a straight line
straight with no chaser
I drunk the Kool-Aid for creatives
and felt the agony of a genius
no one understands
overstands
or comes close to being original
fight or flight syndrome
sounds like an epidemic for quick fixes
and a symptom of things gone bad
bad meaning good.....in abstraction you know

the shape of things to come
a rebirth of failures
I learn to give CPR
and breathe new life into the medium
if life imitates art
then I can only draw from one conclusion
that which continues to paint
into infinity

now picture
the thoughts that bleed
on paper
as we free ourselves
from ourselves

Demonstration

Now picture
the thoughts that bleed on paper
as we free ourselves
from ourselves

just think
of how we can workshop
the kinks and straighten out our imaginations
the idea of being present
not in dreams but in reality

become open to possibilities
of the creator as we create
one in the same
yet
different as fingerprints
a touching sentiment
this ain't about looking good
to feel perfect

what does the soul bare in color
the secret to success
which is you learn more in failure
process driven
with nowhere to go.

Impasto

Process driven with nowhere to go
her thunder thighs clap sound
then, tremble clouds to rain down
color
even her fat back
is greasy meat on bones
stout, dark and rich
with a wealth of knowledge
at her fingertips
melanin caked on
chocolate dripping off her swaying hips
muted shades of brown
with the sun as her crown
tip top shape
her mountain peaks rip
her hair waves to the sea
anytime she cries
cheeks turn desert dry
no matter if I wipe away her valley lows
canvas the sky
and find a rainbow
her mood will climate change
because she guilt trips
Damn!
Mother Nature lays it on thick

Acrylics

Mother Nature lays it on thick
sculpts out of recycled plastics
dilutes pools of murky water
guides palette knives
rinses color away
the brush skinny dips

pigment dries
twice as fast
a charade of oil
but thinner
the truth is in the details
if done correctly

you will never tell
the medium
between the rich man's walls
and the poor man's elixir

Pantone

The medium
between the rich man's walls
and the poor man's elixir
color of the year
black everything 28-1963
the end

Three

FAITH
IS
MY
CANVAS

Stretched Canvas

The shape of things to come
stress and tightened muscles
stretch unprimed pocketbooks
canvas debt in the morning

reflection deeper than wells
painting on a good face
morning rituals for worker bees
heading out the door

wearing depression like cheap cologne
in a lunch bag, bare minimum
and what minimum wage affords
rice, beans and over-fried brains
scrambled worse than bad reception
bread not included

Monday to Friday routine
get up, get home and get a reality check
deliver me a pink slip
because this job is cancerous
and the price of healthcare is sickening

taught to accept circumstance
America must be lactose intolerant
fed crumbs instead of milk and honey

A Page Out of the Journal

Fed crumbs instead of milk and honey
I am onto something BIG
something that will define my career
I am onto something
despite sold signs and likes

I am onto something I can only imagine
and hope will become a reality
and not a dream
in a time of solitude
I am onto something
new and renewed
I am onto something
that feels right
and feels like
one step closer to freedom

I am onto something that I can't put my finger on
but feel where no human hand can touch
I am onto something real
really, I am onto something
that I can't quite articulate
I am onto something within me

Art & Culture

I am onto something within me
returning to empty space and blank walls
between still life and action painting
between color theory and blank canvases
you find a composition

outside of folk art and sculpture
outside of performance and fine brushes
you find an original

in the dark room and a light box
in mixed media and dimensions
you find a movement

in the fire of a kiln
in the textile
designed by a village loom
you find public art

Freelance

You find public art
creates this thing called interpretation
and a chance to be great
can we employ success
necessary to my survival
failure comes with the greatest surprise
the world needs me
finding purpose in existence
out of my mouth
a joyful noise is made
color me sound
mantra is life found in ohm

Commission

Mantra is life found in ohm
maybe it is a concept
this illusive air
flowing in and out
currency that is currently standing in still waters
not grown on trees
instead in growing wants and desires

building wealth on egos
a foundation cemented on privilege
pay close attention, we all have bills to pay
and the play bill, is a one person act
titled: "broke"

find your light

either you are letting your light shine
or trying to find the limelight
the question becomes
how do you keep the lights on?

Creativity

How do you keep the lights on?
the work never ends
sleepless nights and daydreams
finding my voice in the pen
speaking life into existence
purging social criticism
throwing up protest signs
nauseated with unrest
hung over on revolution

if life is a canvas
and death my brush
I paint eternity
with the stroke of a genius
only to find rest in color
because
mistakes are too much to bear
I assume
it is where
my blessings go to hibernate
between a rock
and a hard place
God
shoot it to me straight
where do I go from here?

I Quit (Full-Time Artist)

Where do I go from here
long stares subdued with glowing lights
interrupted by endless clicks
a soundtrack to white noise
in the distance
a sea of bowed heads
cubicle synagogues
here, the complacent worship false idols
corner windows separate rank and position
inhabitants escape to water coolers
discussing strategy and politics
make no mistake
this is a wasteland where souls go to die
cut from a different cloth
nonconformists are labeled traitors
swaddled with patronized promises
fashioning the idea of freedom
take the perp walk
left to pack dreams in cardboard boxes
mail my last check
to consequences and regret

Unemployment

Mail my last check
to consequences and regret
so much of the past
I wish I could delete
trapped
waiting to be set free
no catch and release
America is a zoo
or either a circus
the ringleader is white Jesus
heard he saves

Inspired By

Heard he saves
growing up black in the South
the bible belt
whipped us into shape
marching
bye-and-bye
protesting and confessing our struggles
in wingtips
munching on chips and soda water
blazed a path
until we caught fire
penny candy in hand
lying under trees
to escape the sun
and watchful eyes
the village consoling cries
wiping away tears
as cousins flee north
to big cities up yonder
these days
still amazed how Mama and dem
be sitting on the porch
waving at old folks
repast bye-and-bye

Space

Waving at old folks repast
bye-and-bye
left more than memories
stories of other galaxies
told in jazz music
and comic books
we read pictures
lied about
who we wanted to become
for fear
of where we wanted to go
our futures lingered
heavier than anxiety
from past due bills
later settling
on polyester couches
a place family gathered
now collecting dust
but still holds up
to aunties laughter
and Uncle Bo's knees
plastic monuments
trophies from little league
stand tall
similar to cousins back-to-back
and shoulder-to-shoulder
next to the record player

a Crown Royal bag sits
filled with dominoes
the epitome of cool
in the background
vinyl spinning Sun-Ra
and Headhunters
from the Atlantic to Afrofuturism
a galaxy of midnight blues
years later
I would discover
interpretations of black space
trying to keep pace
moving me sonically

Pattern

Moving me sonically
raced down to radio programming
tuned into stereotypes
listened for my cue
and heard
rhythms
the blues, gospel and funk
plus, hip hop, soul and jazz thumped
turning off exploitation and turning up culture
life pumps in my veins
born with a beating drum

surfing for mental currents
across wavelengths
we danced into the night
feet weary
our journey not choreographed
so, we met destiny in the horn section
until angels sang
and at that moment
we heard heaven
electrified
sending shockwaves
as silence filled the air
then, right when we found our groove
someone decided to unplug freedom

Artist Statement

Someone decided to unplug freedom
turn down all that bippity bop
talk in rhyme
pivot on the dime
swinging on breakbeats
call
and the response
can I kick it
yes, you can

personas battle egos
ink flows over pages
rhythm scratching
usher in a new sound
faces fade
to black and earth brown

for the record
this vibration and energy
considered savagery
let the beast loose
and the youth, take turns
recording history
with a tape and boombox

dreaming of ways to escape
concrete jungles

remain humble and demand more
block parties, inspire bodies to move
built on culture
one nation under a groove
fighting the power
while crews hunt
on the prowl
preying over poor souls
to move the crowd

gather around
street poets
untamed lyrics go wild
universal sound
of yes, yes, y'all
to the beat y'all
bound to the loop
complete the cypha
their stories told on buildings
by graffiti writers
all heading uptown
the day Mother Earth
gave birth to hip-hop
and it don't stop
and it don't quit
and it don't stop
and it don't quit

enters the room
Ma 'Dukes with a shoe

she can't sleep
cause my favorite rap song is on repeat

Color Palette

Cause my favorite rap song is on repeat
record crackling
add hot sauce for flavor
give me some skin
hi fives and jive cousins
worth less than two dead flies
southern fried
more luster than aunties gold tooth
letting our little light shine
lucky number is the dozens
holy rollers
with thunder laughter
scripture and lies
under sheepish eyes
at night
the sky is filled with rhythm and blues
where old folk smiles
are broken into
like leather shoes
worn down
over soul food
more to offer
and even more to give
down here with Magnolia trees
country roads
and hot water cornbread
where we live

we return to innocence
the color of dirt
given to me since birth

Red

Given to me since birth
not cherry or strawberry
at chicken shacks
we ask for red drank and toast
with everything
bologna sandwiches
hair grease
and stain guts with color
so good, we break out in song
cheers to the flavor of black childhood

Barbershop Talk

Cheers to the flavor of black childhood
booster seats and capes
for unsung heroes
safe space for blackness
politics fade into cuts

deep how jokes pass around
lunch plates and street game
bootleg items exchanged
not the circus
but get clowned

newcomers receive stares
checkered linoleum floors, add decor
on the wall, black icons
typically, you make appointments
but wait for hours
especially after cigarette breaks

most employees done time
switching barbers is a crime
where married men escape

relationships built tighter than naps
generations take seats
on thrones
wannabes lie about

who they boned

be sure to leave a tip
if not, your fresh cut
may be suited for a cap

domino games
where onlookers keep score
old timers nodding off
stats and opinions
always given
room full of coaches
mix red cups
musk and oil sheen
vice is dialogue
and who can ball
elders speak scripture
blue collar to degreed
feel free to grab a seat
with clippers
buzzing in ears
that's why I've been coming here
for years

Kitchen Blues

That's why I've been coming here for years
getting back to my roots
with no Alex Haley
located below an acreage of naps
Afro picks massage scalps
and tame new growth
tightly wrapped and coiled, naturally resistant
the revolution begins

when strains throw up their hands
and lay down
not willing to surrender but retreat
to a rough patch
as if my hair fell off the wagon
maybe allergic to grease
and the fire of lye
when left on too long
burning to comb thru the struggle
to find peace
in the back of my mind
and next to my neck, something is cooking
my kitchen under construction
in need of a remodel

Detroit Landscape

My kitchen under construction
in need of a remodel
trading records for manicured lawns
steel faces covered in sweat
plywood windows and burned lots
a city once brown bombed
America's engine gone bankrupt
amongst construction boots and gators
tooling around soulful sounds
manufactured hope, amongst black dreams
once abandoned, turned grassy green
as the white man tries to Mo-the-town

Gentrification

As the white man tries to mow the town
in front yards
for sale signs
come with murals and coffee shops
a refuge for luminaries and soccer moms
skip salutations
maybe they were raised different
there is an air about them
replacing streetwear for workout tights
amiss are LL Cool J
around the way girls
double-dutching
with corner store pickles
weighed down by age
and laundry mat change
grandmothers move to the side
for strollers and small dogs

make way for knockoffs
they are so pastiche
when it comes to melanin chiefs
replacing Pocahontas with Cinderellas and Madonnas
God bless the child
that got his rent-to-own

life on lay-a-way
learning how to pay

as you go
pass jail
with 10,000 steps
community activist
locked up and locked in arms
linked like herringbones
around blue collar necks
gritty streets riddled with potholes, cooking slang
a cool kid's bread and butter
an exchange of words, heard as microaggressions
told remain cool
by old heads
who move
to blaxploitation soundtracks
it ain't what it used to be

searching for better days
we stand on corners
listening to wisdom
patrons of liquor stores and lottery tickets
hood flaneurs
loiter as new neighbors pass
there is an impasse
change is needed
people displaced

for those
riding into the sunset
heard MLK Blvd. got a new bike path
now architecture

built for suburban archetypes
designed out of red lines
the inner city
revised and edited
can't blame high rent
on bad credit
where do we belong

Sold (Ballin!)

Where do we belong? Holding court. We stretch our imagination and jump over struggles. Learn the difference between position and posturing. Flying above clouds with Nike Airs on feet. Practice religiously. Sweat pours from our rubber souls. Black bodies bounce around ideas and set screens. While society offers a full court press. Throw hardwood on the fire to keep thoughts warm. Need vision to see the point, so we pray at the top of the key. Palming destiny without a care in the world. These conditions cause minds to travel. Globetrotting, but ain't never left the hood. In the end, it seems we all have the same dream. Everybody wants to win. With seconds on the clock, looking for the rock and God to open doors. Life gives a hard foul, which sends us to the stripe. A mark of brilliance and testament to sacrifice. Drive the lane. We run and gun. Taking off with false starts. Hopes and dreams shift into park. Even our goals are chained. Failures we block out. Stand on corners to take shots. Waiting to be picked. Writing new narratives. First-drafted by the streets. We do it all for a rep, so tell me who got next?

ABOUT THE AUTHOR

Rosie Lee is a multi-talented artist, writer, scholar, and hip-hop aficionado. At the age of sixteen, Lee began his career as a poet performing with a nationally recognized spoken-word collective. As an educator and artist, Lee attempts to bridge his love for art and culture through storytelling. Lee has become a renaissance man with a dandy fresh style and peculiar name. A collector of vintage bikes, jazz records, and books add to his sense of adventure and imagination.

Get to know the author at www.rosieleewrites.com

Made in the USA
Coppell, TX
05 July 2022

79584373R00053